CW01510001

Original title:
Yondered Blossoms Beneath the Faerie Knob

Author: Liisi Lendorav
ISBN HARDBACK: 978-1-80559-384-3
ISBN PAPERBACK: 978-1-80559-883-1

# A Reverent Dance of Petals and Stars

In the moonlight's soft embrace,
Petals sway in quiet grace,
Stars above blink with delight,
Illuminating the night.

A whisper of the zephyr's call,
Spirals round the garden wall,
While shadows stretch and play,
In this sacred ballet.

Each bloom tells a tale of old,
Of love's warmth and dreams bold,
As orchids twirl and roses sigh,
Beneath the vast, velvet sky.

Dancing with the fireflies' glow,
Nature's symphony in flow,
A reverent hush falls near,
As secrets of the night appear.

In this garden, time stands still,
Each petal dancing at its will,
In the harmony of night and day,
A reverent dance, bright and gay.

# The Swaying Song of Sylvan Bloom

In the heart of the woodland green,
Where sunlight filters, soft and keen,
Flora hums a gentle tune,
Beneath the watchful, silver moon.

With each breeze, the blossoms sway,
In a rhythm that will not stray,
Nature's chorus weaves and weaves,
Through the branches, as it breathes.

Primrose nods and daisies spin,
Caressed by whispers, soft within,
Echoing secrets old and true,
In the depths of morning dew.

From shadows deep to valleys bright,
The blooms dance with pure delight,
In the sanctuary of trees,
Where all hearts are gently pleased.

Silent echoes of pure bliss,
In every leaf, a tender kiss,
The swaying song from shadows' home,
Calls every soul to wander, roam.

# Whims of Flora's Hidden Realm

In a garden tucked away,
Where the petals dance and play,
Whims of flora weave a tale,
As secrets in the breeze set sail.

Each bud a promise yet to bloom,
Unfolding dreams without a gloom,
Colors burst in wild array,
In this realm where shadows sway.

Softly whispers the lavender,
As daisies dance and do confer,
While ferns curl in sweet refrain,
A playful secret left unchained.

In murmurs of the evening light,
A symphony of pure delight,
With every sigh and gentle swirl,
Magic dwells in this hidden world.

Here, every flower knows its role,
In whimsical ballet, they console,
Nature's laughter fills the air,
In the hidden realm, beyond compare.

# Colors Colliding in the Dreaming Wood

Beneath the canopy so wide,
A spectrum blooms, where secrets hide.
Crimson whispers, emerald sighs,
In shadows bright, the color flies.

A dance of light on leaves of gold,
Stories of nature gently told.
The blue of dusk, the white of dawn,
In this wood, all fears are gone.

Violet blooms that softly glow,
In twilight dreams, their magic flows.
A canvas vast, a painted night,
Where colors clash, igniting light.

Through tangled roots, the spirits weave,
In hues unseen, they dare to believe.
A prism formed from joy and strife,
In dreaming wood, we find our life.

# Pathways of Jasmine and Twilight

In evening's glow, the jasmine crawls,
Its fragrance dances through the halls.
Twilight drapes its purple shawl,
As whispers echo, softly call.

Along the paths where shadows creep,
The secrets of the night we keep.
With every step, enchantment found,
In jasmine's breath, the heart resounds.

Moonlight weaves through branches bare,
Casting dreams upon the air.
Each petal holds a tale to tell,
Of love and loss, of heaven and hell.

The twilight beckons, secrets shared,
Through fragrant trails, we are ensnared.
In this moment, pure and true,
Pathways merge, me and you.

## Legends Born of Magical Flora

In valleys deep, the legends grow,
From roots of tales, the stories flow.
Each petal holds a timeless grace,
A magic realm, a sacred space.

The elder tree, with wisdom vast,
Whispers of the ancient past.
From flower's bloom, the spirits rise,
In fragrant dreams, the truth belies.

The clover sings of fortune near,
While lilies chant what hearts hold dear.
In petals soft, enchantments gleam,
Creating stories from a dream.

With every breeze, a fable spins,
In gardens where the magic begins.
Our history, through flora learned,
The tales of life, forever burned.

# The Faerie's Garden of Memory

In a garden where the whispers play,
The faerie's light guides the way.
Among the blooms, with gentle grace,
Each memory finds its sacred place.

A tapestry of moments shared,
In petals soft, our dreams are bared.
With every bud that opens wide,
A piece of time, where dreams reside.

The daisies dance in summer's glow,
Where secrets of the heart can flow.
In twilight's arms, the stories blend,
In nature's dance, we find our end.

Through fragrant paths, the memories roam,
In the faerie's arms, we find our home.
A garden rich with love's embrace,
In every flower, we trace our place.

# Whispered Tales of the Floral Realm

In the garden's soft embrace,
Secrets bloom with gentle grace.
Petals whisper to the air,
Fragrant tales of love and care.

Bees hum softly, wings a-flutter,
While sunlight warms the fragrant butter.
Each blossom holds a hidden sigh,
A fleeting glance that drifts nearby.

Dewdrops shine like tiny stars,
Glistening dreams from near and far.
Mornings weave their tales anew,
In colors rich, in every hue.

Wind's soft whisper through the trees,
Carries scents upon the breeze.
Nature's ink on paper leaves,
Writes stories that the heart believes.

Underneath the arching boughs,
Magic lurks as deep as vows.
Every petal, soft and true,
Whispers secrets just for you.

# Hidden Realms of Fragrant Wonders

Beneath the shade of ancient oaks,
Lies a world where nature pokes.
Fungi glow in twilight's gleam,
And breezes carry a fragrant dream.

Vines entwine like lovers' hands,
Hidden realms in enchanted lands.
Every leaf a story spins,
Of laughter lost and hidden sins.

Through thickets dense, the heart will race,
In secret corners, dreams embrace.
Floral scents weave through the air,
A tapestry of love laid bare.

Whispers echo in the night,
As shadows dance in soft moonlight.
Petals drifting like lost sighs,
As time unravels and softly flies.

Beneath the stars, a symphony,
Of fragrance, freedom, harmony.
In every bloom and every shade,
Hidden wonders unafraid.

### The Dance of Faerie Ferns and Flowers

In forests deep where shadows play,
Faeries twirl at close of day.
With silver dust and laughter's cheer,
They weave their magic, ever near.

Ferns unfurl like secrets told,
In moonlit glades, their dance unfolds.
Petals sway to an unseen tune,
As night blooms soft 'neath a silver moon.

Glimmers spark in the fragrant night,
While blossoms sway, a wondrous sight.
Beams of glow from starlit skies,
Guide the faeries as they rise.

They beckon ferns to join the cheer,
Inviting all to draw quite near.
A harmony of earth and light,
In every dance, pure delight.

Through tangled vines, they laugh and spin,
With joyful songs that rise within.
In the magic of wildflowers,
Faeries dance through endless hours.

# Enchantment in the Garden's Breath

In the garden, life abounds,
Nature's whispers fill the grounds.
A symphony of sights and scents,
Where every moment's magic hints.

Butterflies flit like painted dreams,
Through petals kissed by sunlit beams.
Fragrant roses curl and lean,
In a world where all is green.

Branches sway in gentle raves,
Crickets sing from hidden caves.
The breeze, a soft caressing sigh,
Brings sweet aromas drifting by.

Garden beds hold stories old,
Of love and loss, of dreams retold.
Each blossom a chapter new,
Each leaf a promise bright and true.

As twilight falls, the colors blend,
In shadows where the wonders end.
The garden breathes in night's embrace,
As starlit spells fill every space.

## Chants of the Blossoms Untold

In gardens where whispers dwell,
Petals weave a hidden spell.
Soft melodies kiss the air,
As nature sings without a care.

Beneath the arches, colors dance,
Each bloom a note, a sweet romance.
Swaying gently, hearts entwined,
With every breath, the world's confined.

The sun dips low, a golden hue,
As twilight night brings dreams anew.
Silent shouts of joy cascade,
In every shadow, light is made.

Stars awaken in the night,
Their twinkling bright, a guiding light.
Each blossom hums a silent tune,
As night embraces them in swoon.

In every petal lies a song,
Whispers of where we all belong.
Chants of blossoms unfold near,
A symphony brought to our ear.

## Blossoms Bow Beneath Starlit Skies

Underneath the cosmic dome,
Blossoms bow, their fragrant home.
With every rustle, secrets shared,
In starlit nights, all hearts are bared.

Moonlight bathes the world in grace,
Petals glisten, nature's face.
Each fragrant breeze a tender sigh,
As dreams unfold beneath the sky.

The nightingale, its song so pure,
Calls forth magic, calm and sure.
Blossoms sway with gentle ease,
In symphony with swaying trees.

Night whispers soft through leafy lanes,
As silver droplets kiss the plains.
Nature's breath, a soft caress,
In quiet moments, we find rest.

Blossoms bow, the stars align,
In twilight's glow, our souls entwine.
United under vast expanse,
A world reborn in sacred dance.

### The Lure of the Fluttering Foliage

Leaves murmur tales in calming hues,
Breath of the wind, nature's muse.
Dancing lightly, soft and free,
Fluttering whispers call to me.

Golden sunlight filters through,
Patterns shifting, a vibrant view.
Colors merge, a gentle sway,
Nature's canvas, bright and gay.

Each rustling leaf, a story told,
Of seasons past, of dreams unfold.
A tapestry of green and gold,
In every hue, a memory bold.

The dance continues, wild and bright,
Drawing eyes to nature's light.
Foliage beckons with gentle charm,
In its embrace lies a calming balm.

So let us wander through this place,
Where foliage glows with timeless grace.
In every flutter, joy is found,
Nature's lure, a love profound.

# Tangles of Light in Blooming Shadows

In shadows deep, where secrets dwell,
Light weaves patterns, a magic spell.
Blooming flowers in twilight glow,
Tangles of light begin to grow.

The garden hums a soft refrain,
Colorful strokes, a bright domain.
Sunbeams flicker, shadows play,
In this dance of night and day.

Whispers linger in the air,
Petals fold, a tender prayer.
In the hush of fading light,
Mary's bloom ignites the night.

Where blossoms intertwine and weave,
Each corner hums, a tale to believe.
Tangles of light, shadows embrace,
Nature's beauty, a soft grace.

Let your heart be light and free,
Among the blooms, come dance with me.
In this garden, dreams align,
In blooming shadows, love will shine.

## Moonlit Elegance in Flora's Grasp

In gardens hushed beneath the glow,
The moonlight weaves a silver thread,
It whispers secrets soft and low,
As shadows dance on petals spread.

A breeze carries the night's perfume,
While blossoms sway, a gentle tune,
In silken hues, the shadows bloom,
Bathed in the glow of a tender moon.

Each flower tells a tale anew,
Of love and loss in twilight hours,
In every shade, a hint of dew,
Embracing night with whispered powers.

The stars align in symphony,
As crickets sing their serenade,
In this embrace of mystery,
The night unfolds a soft cascade.

Moonlit elegance, a soft caress,
In Flora's grasp, the world stands still,
In nature's art, we find our rest,
Amongst the dreams the night fulfills.

## Threads of Enchantment in Blossom Winds

The daisies twirl in playful gusts,
Spinning tales of time and grace,
In every petal, a promise trust,
A dance so light, a sweet embrace.

Through fields of gold, the wildflowers sway,
While whispers of enchantment flow,
In twilight's glow, they softly play,
A gentle hymn, a secret show.

Beneath the boughs where shadows creep,
The moonbeams sprinkle silver threads,
In every hue, the night will keep,
The magic spun where silence spreads.

A tapestry of colors blend,
As nature's breath brings life anew,
In every corner, dreams transcend,
Wrapped in fragrant blossoms' view.

Threads of enchantment weave the air,
In every bloom, a story blooms,
Through blossom winds, beyond compare,
In nature's heart, our spirit looms.

# Ethereal Gardens of Forgotten Tales

In gardens rich with whispers deep,
Where ancient echoes softly sigh,
The petals guard their secrets keep,
Beneath the watchful, starlit sky.

The willows sway with tales untold,
Of lovers lost to time's embrace,
In every shade, a story bold,
Through every turn, we trace their grace.

Amidst the herbs, the silence stirs,
A gentle hush, a moment's breath,
In every leaf, the past concurs,
A garden cradling life and death.

The violets blush with memories sweet,
Of laughter shared in seasons' flow,
In twilight's warmth, our souls will meet,
In realms where dreams and dangers grow.

Ethereal gardens, timeless and vast,
In every flower, a flicker reigns,
Forgotten tales will ever last,
In nature's arms, our heart remains.

# The Faerie's Field of Dancing Iris

In fields where irises sway and twirl,
The faerie's magic starts to sing,
Amidst the blooms, a joyful whirl,
With laughter light as morning's wing.

Colors flutter in the bright sunlight,
Each petal spins a lively tale,
With whispers soft, a sweet delight,
As faeries weave through every trail.

The sun dips low behind the trees,
While shadows fall in dusky hues,
In this place, where time's at ease,
The iris blooms sing out their blues.

With fleeting grace, they dance around,
In circles bright, they paint the air,
In joyous steps, no sadness found,
In every breath, a dream to share.

The faerie's field, a wondrous sight,
Where every glance ignites the sky,
In dancing irises, pure light,
A spell of joy will never die.

## Blooming Dreams in the Starlit Vale

In the vale where starlight drips,
Dreams unfurl on silken lips.
Petals whisper tales of night,
Guided by the moon's soft light.

Breezes carry scents so sweet,
Guiding hearts with gentle beat.
Underneath the cosmic glow,
Nature's secrets begin to flow.

Each bloom dances in the dark,
Flickers bright, a hidden spark.
Hope ignites in colors bold,
Stories waiting to be told.

In this realm where wishes soar,
Life awakens at the core.
Hands outstretched to catch the dreams,
Floating softly on silver beams.

With each breath, the night ignites,
Awakening forgotten sights.
In the vale where shadows gleam,
Hearts entwined in blooming dream.

# Phantom Fragrance of the Woods

Through the trees, a whisper sighs,
Phantom scents where silence lies.
Misty trails of unknown grace,
Linger softly in this place.

Beneath the boughs, the shadows hum,
Nature's secrets, sweetly come.
Hints of spice and earthy tones,
Carried by the ancient stones.

Amidst the ferns, a fleeting breeze,
Carries echoes of the trees.
Every step reveals a tale,
In the woods where dreams prevail.

Moonlight dances on the stream,
Reflecting every hidden dream.
Every fragrance tells a lore,
Of the woods we can explore.

In the twilight, shadows wake,
Nature stirs and hearts shall quake.
Breathe it in, the phantom air,
Feel the magic hanging there.

# Veiled Fluttering in the Thicket

In the thicket, shadows play,
Veiled fluttering lights the way.
Wings of gold and hints of blue,
Come alive in morning dew.

Hidden worlds in every turn,
Mysteries of life discern.
Gentle whispers in the leaves,
Speak of nature's soft reprieves.

Through the blooms, the fairies roam,
Guiding hearts to find a home.
Every moment, pure delight,
Veiled in the embrace of night.

Colors shift as day breaks free,
Painting dreams on bough and tree.
In the thicket, joy takes flight,
Hints of magic, pure and bright.

With each step, the pathways blend,
Nature's wonders never end.
Veiled flutterings, soft and shy,
Open hearts to the sky.

# Unraveled Mysteries of Flora

In the garden, secrets hide,
Unraveled mysteries abide.
Petals curled like whispers true,
Each one tells a tale anew.

Vines entwined in soft embrace,
Cover ground with gentle grace.
Every leaf, a story spun,
Of the life that's just begun.

Beneath the blooms, a world alive,
Nature's dance where dreams derive.
Colors burst in joyful cheer,
Unlocking wonders hidden near.

In the twilight, shadows creep,
Carrying secrets that we keep.
Every fragrance, sharp and sweet,
Guiding wanderers to their feet.

With each glance, the heart explores,
Unraveled mysteries of Shores.
In the flora's calm embrace,
Life resides in every space.

# Dreams Weaved in Celestial Petals

In the gardens where whispers dwell,
Each petal holds a secret spell.
Under starlight's tender gaze,
Dreams unfolding in gentle ways.

Softly painted in shades of night,
The universe shines warm and bright.
Woven tales in silken threads,
For the dreamers, where fate treads.

In the quiet, where time suspends,
Hope and magic; matter bends.
With every breath, the cosmos sighs,
As dreams take flight beneath the skies.

Nature's brushstrokes, vivid hues,
Carving moments we can choose.
Celestial bloom in every heart,
Bearing wishes that won't depart.

In these gardens, forever ours,
Dancing gently with the stars.
As dreams are weaved, we gently roam,
Finding in petals our way home.

# Echoes in the Flower-filled Glade

In a glade where flowers sing,
Echoes of laughter take wing.
Petals dance in the soft breeze,
Whispering secrets among the trees.

Sunlight filters through the leaves,
A tapestry that nature weaves.
Each bloom tells a story bright,
In colors kissed by morning light.

The breeze carries a fragrant tune,
Filled with promise, morning's boon.
A chorus of life, rich and sweet,
In this haven, hearts skip a beat.

With every step, a new delight,
Where shadows meet the softest light.
Nature's embrace, a soothing balm,
In the glade, life feels so calm.

Echoes linger in the air,
Moments captured, beyond compare.
In this flower-filled retreat,
Our souls find solace, pure and sweet.

# Mystique of the Vivid Thicket

In the thicket, shadows twine,
Mysteries hidden, secrets shine.
Leaves like jewels, bright and bold,
Each twist reveals a tale untold.

Underbrush teems with life unseen,
Where sunlight weaves through lush green.
Whispers linger, old and wise,
Echoing through these wild skies.

The air is thick with wonder's breath,
In every corner, hints of depth.
Nature's canvas, painted wild,
In the heart, we are beguiled.

Startling sights, colors collide,
In the thicket, our fears subside.
Adventure calls with each soft step,
Into the magic, we're adept.

Mystique swirls in the evening light,
As day unfolds to cloak of night.
In the thicket's embrace so vast,
We find our souls, anchored fast.

## Spirits Amidst the Twilight Orchards

In orchards where the twilight breathes,
Spirits dance among the leaves.
Ripening fruits in dusky glow,
Whispers carried soft and low.

Beneath the boughs, shadows play,
As light begins to fade away.
The night unfolds a mystic song,
In harmony, we all belong.

Branches sway with stories old,
Fables etched in bark and gold.
In this realm where silence flows,
The heart awakens, gently grows.

The air is thick with sweet perfume,
As twilight blooms in softening gloom.
Spirits linger, sharing tales,
Of timeless paths and gentle trails.

With a hush, the world holds its breath,
In orchards, life confronts its depth.
Embraced by night, we find our part,
In these shadows, we mend our heart.

## Echoing Lullabies Among the Blossoms

In gardens where soft whispers sigh,
Beneath the dance of bluebird's flight,
Lullabies weave through the lilac highs,
Cradling dreams in the velvet night.

Moonlight glistens on petals wide,
Each bloom a story, fresh and bright,
Through fragrant paths, gentle hearts glide,
Finding solace in nature's light.

The breeze hums tales of love's embrace,
Rocking the world in sweet delight,
Among the blooms, a sacred space,
Where soft echoes blend with the night.

Stars twirl above in silent grace,
Casting shadows that dance with glee,
A lullaby finds its perfect place,
In the heart of the blossoming tree.

So let the night cradle your dreams,
Where the flowers whisper and sigh,
In the garden's hush, nothing seems,
To echo louder than love's soft cry.

# Fantasies Blooming Underneath the Stars

Under a cloak of twilight's sigh,
Fantasies awaken with the night,
Shooting stars paint the velvet sky,
As dreams take root in moon's soft light.

In the fields where shadows blend,
Whispers of magic softly play,
Each twinkle, a promise, a blend,
Of hopes that bloom and sway.

The world is hushed, a secret place,
Where thoughts can wander, free to roam,
Time slips by in a timeless grace,
As night wraps us in its sweet dome.

Each breath is filled with a wish's gleam,
Stars gather close to hear the call,
We chase the moon, lost in our dream,
Beneath the blanket of nightfall.

Hand in hand, we dance through night,
In realms where fantasies ignite,
Underneath the starry height,
Every moment feels just right.

# The Realm of Whispered Petals

In the realm where petals whisper,
Every breeze carries a tender sigh,
The flowers speak in colors crisper,
Telling tales of love that fly.

Dancing through the fields of bloom,
With sweetness heavy in the air,
The world embraced in nature's room,
With every turn, the heart laid bare.

In this garden of wishes spun,
Soft shadows linger, light and free,
Every petal kissed by the sun,
Writes stories meant for you and me.

Evening falls like a silken shroud,
Wrapping whispers in olden lore,
While laughter ripples, soft yet loud,
In the realm where hearts can soar.

So linger here, let moments blend,
Where whispered petals call your name,
In this paradise where dreams transcend,
Life blooms bright, love's gentle flame.

## Veils of Color in Shape and Wind

Veils of color dance with the breeze,
Painting stories in the evening light,
Shadows play among the trees,
As day gives way to starry night.

In gentle swirls, the fabric flows,
Soft whispers twirl in playful flight,
Colors emerge as twilight glows,
Merging daydreams with endless night.

Each hue a note in nature's song,
Crafting tapestries rich and grand,
As one by one, the stars belong,
To a symphony across the land.

Through this canvas, winds do weave,
Stories forgotten long ago,
In this dance, we dare believe,
That dreams once lost can surely grow.

So let the colors take you far,
To places where your spirit's free,
In veils of wonder, be the star,
In shape and wind, find all you seek.

## Shadows and Petals in Secret Paths

In twilight's gentle, hushed embrace,
Petals fall with silent grace.
Shadows dance beneath the trees,
Whispers float upon the breeze.

Paths entwined in nature's care,
Secret worlds beyond compare.
Lilies bloom where shadows play,
In the dusk, a soft ballet.

Glimmers of a hidden light,
Guide the footsteps of the night.
Every petal tells a tale,
As the moon begins to sail.

Beneath the stars, the echoes sing,
Of all the joy the night can bring.
In the garden, dreams take flight,
Holding close the heart's delight.

And as the dawn begins to break,
Awakening from night's sweet lake,
Shadows fade in golden hue,
While petals whisper secrets true.

## Serenade of the Whispering Blooms

In meadows lush with vibrant hues,
A serenade that nature brews.
Gentle winds caress the leaves,
Whispers soft as twilight weaves.

Each flower sways with sweet delight,
A melody that warms the night.
The daisies laugh, the roses sigh,
As the stars twinkle in the sky.

Moonlight kisses every petal,
In this dream, our hearts shall settle.
With every note in soft refrain,
The earth hums softly, free from pain.

Crickets' song and owl's hoot,
Join the blooms in their pursuit.
Together they create a spell,
In nature's choir, all is well.

As dawn ignites the waking land,
Fleeting dreams slip through our hands.
Yet in the day, their echoes stay,
In every bloom, a love bouquet.

# Floral Secrets of the Moon's Caress

Beneath the moon's soft silver light,
Floral secrets take their flight.
In gardens deep with shades of night,
Mysteries bloom, pure and bright.

Petals whisper, tales unfold,
Of nights spent in dreams of old.
In shadows' arms, they softly sway,
Guardians of what words can't say.

Each blossom holds a gleaming dream,
Shimmering in the lunar beam.
In twilight's embrace, stories spin,
Of magic lost and found within.

The nightingale sings to the stars,
As petals dance free of scars.
Wrapped in a veil of cosmic lace,
Every bloom holds a warm embrace.

As dawn arrives, the secrets wane,
Yet in the heart, they will remain.
For every petal kissed by night,
Holds a promise, pure delight.

# The Embrace of Ethereal Petals

In gardens where the whispers twine,
Ethereal petals, soft and fine.
Their colors blush in morning's glow,
In every breeze, their secrets flow.

Dancing lightly, spirits rise,
Underneath the vast blue skies.
With each touch of the sun's warm hand,
Joy awakens in the land.

In twilight's calm, their fragrance spreads,
Entwining dreams within our heads.
Delicate, like thoughts of bliss,
Every petal holds a wish.

As night enfolds the waking world,
In a tapestry, they're swirled.
Wrapped in moonlight's soft embrace,
Nature's heart finds its true place.

And when the dawn breaks fresh and free,
The petals whisper joyfully.
In every bloom, a heart concealed,
In nature's love, our fate revealed.

## Enchanted Sketches on Petal Canvas

Delicate strokes in soft decay,
Petals whisper secrets of the day,
Colors blend in twilight's kiss,
A silent dance, a fleeting bliss.

Nature's palette, wide and true,
Each hue a memory, fresh as dew,
Sketches drawn with sunlit grace,
In this garden, time finds space.

A breeze carries dreams aloft,
Echoes of laughter, warm and soft,
Brushing close, the edges fade,
In this canvas, love is laid.

Through the shadows, light shall gleam,
Each petal holds a hidden dream,
Artistry in each gentle fold,
Stories of the heart unfold.

Beneath the stars, the night extends,
In blooming silence, magic bends,
Eternal sketches, pure and bright,
Awakening in the moonlight.

# The Symphony of Wandering Blooms

A gentle breeze begins to play,
Flowers sway in sun's warm ray,
Notes of fragrance fill the air,
Nature sings without a care.

Petals flutter, colors blend,
Each bloom a story, time to spend,
Whispers soft, a playful tune,
In gardens rich beneath the moon.

The orchestra of life unfolds,
In wild patterns, beauty molds,
Dancing spirits twirl and glide,
In harmony, the world abides.

Melodies of joy and peace,
In nature's heart, all troubles cease,
Strumming chords of pure delight,
In every bud, the world ignites.

As twilight hums its sweet refrain,
A symphony of blooms sustain,
Resonating in every soul,
Weaving dreams that make us whole.

### Flickers of Magic in the Flowerbed

In flowerbeds where shadows play,
Whispers of magic dance and sway,
Tiny sparks in petals bright,
Illuminate the velvet night.

Softly twinkling, dreams arise,
Hidden wonders in disguise,
Awakened by the moon's soft glow,
Each bloom a tale, a story flow.

Glimmers caught in morning dew,
Secrets shared 'tween me and you,
In this realm where fairies tread,
Flickers of magic lightly spread.

A kingdom where the heart can soar,
Nature's magic, rich galore,
In every bud, in every leaf,
A tapestry beyond belief.

With every petal, light imbues,
Enchanting paths in vibrant hues,
Flickers glow as day departs,
In flowerbeds, we find our hearts.

## Beneath the Gaze of Silvery Petals

Beneath the gaze of silvery blooms,
Whispers echo in sunlit rooms,
Petals soft with a gentle grace,
Embrace the world in quiet space.

In twilight's glow, their beauty shines,
Carving dreams in patterned lines,
Each bloom a wish, a secret shared,
In fragrant sighs, the heart is bared.

The starlit night and petals weave,
A tapestry that we believe,
Fragrant gardens hold our sighs,
Dreamers dance 'neath endless skies.

Fleeting hours, a sacred trust,
In nature's grasp, we linger, must,
With every breeze, a story told,
In silver petals, lives unfold.

Beneath the gaze of nature's heart,
Find solace in each fragrant part,
As silvery blooms in moonlight sway,
We find our own along the way.

# The Faerie's Secret Orchard

In the hush of hidden glades,
Magic whispers through the leaves,
Faeries dance in softest shades,
Where dreams entwine like gentle eaves.

Beneath the boughs of ancient trees,
Elixirs of the night are brewed,
Petals sway in the softest breeze,
In this realm where joys are strewed.

Glimmers of jewels twinkle bright,
A symphony of laughter sings,
The moon casts down her silver light,
As night unveils her mystic wings.

Secrets held in twilight's glow,
Blooming wonders gently sigh,
With every shadow, stories flow,
Forever etched beneath the sky.

In this sacred, sacred place,
Time is lost, and yet it thrives,
The faerie's secret, a soft embrace,
Where nature breathes and love survives.

## Twilight's Lament of Flowering Fates

Beneath the twilight's velvet kiss,
The flowers whisper soft goodbyes,
In hues of gold, a fleeting bliss,
As daylight fades and darkness flies.

Petals droop in sorrowed grace,
Each bloom a tale of joys once spun,
The sun retreats, a slow embrace,
As shadows stretch, the day is done.

In gardens where the echoes dwell,
Fragrant wishes linger near,
The scent of memories, bittersweet spell,
Dances in the twilight cheer.

The stars come forth, a twinkling choir,
In silence they recount the strife,
As night invokes a quiet fire,
To warm the remnants of lost life.

In this lament, the flowers weep,
For what was bright, now softly fades,
Yet in each heart, the shadows keep,
The essence of their fragrant glades.

## A Dreamer's Grove of Silken Sighs

In a grove where dreams take flight,
Whispers weave through branches high,
Silken sighs in the dusky light,
Bathe the world in softest sky.

Dewdrops glisten on emerald leaves,
Where hopes are spun like morning thread,
Nature's heart, the soul receives,
In this tranquil haven spread.

Beneath the arches, twilight falls,
Each shadow dances with the moon,
In quiet corners, wonder calls,
And melodies of night attune.

Every sigh becomes a tale,
Of love and loss and dreams unfurled,
In this rich tapestry, we sail,
Through portals of a hidden world.

Dreamer's grove, where silence reigns,
And magic lingers in the night,
Where every thought, like soft refrains,
Creates the bonds of sweet delight.

# Secrets in the Meadow's Heart

In the meadow where secrets bloom,
A tapestry of colors unfolds,
Whispers rise from the earth's soft womb,
Each petal cradles tales untold.

Here wildflowers sway in sweet dance,
The breeze carries a hidden tune,
Nature's lore gives wings to chance,
Beneath the watchful gaze of moon.

Amidst the grasses, shadows play,
In every rustle, a soft sigh,
The mysteries of night and day,
In chorus weave a lullaby.

A hidden path leads to the soul,
Where the heart finds its sacred thread,
In gentle whispers, dreams console,
As wild desires softly spread.

In this meadow's tender clasp,
Secrets bloom in sunlit grace,
Where every thought and hope can grasp,
The magic held in nature's embrace.

# The Fern's Soft Sighs

In the morning light so bright,
Whispers dance on leaves at height.
Softly swaying in the breeze,
Gentle sighs among the trees.

Nature hums a secret tune,
Crickets' calls beneath the moon.
Ferns know tales of earth and sky,
Their soft voice, a nature's sigh.

Roots entwined in tender soil,
Nurtured by the sun's sweet toil.
Each frond reaching wide and far,
Kissed by dew, a shining star.

In the glade where shadows play,
Ferns hold whispers of the day.
Casting dreams in emerald hue,
Nature's heart, forever true.

As twilight drapes its velvet screen,
Ferns awaken, soft and green.
Breathing secrets to the night,
In their hush, the world feels right.

# In the Shade of Forgotten Trees

Beneath the boughs where sunlight fades,
Whispers linger, time replays.
Mossy carpets hold our dreams,
In their embrace, reality gleams.

Shadows stretch in quiet peace,
Echoes fade, the worries cease.
Branches sway, a gentle song,
Nature's voice where hearts belong.

The stories held in weathered bark,
Of ancient times and journeys stark.
A world once bright with laughter clear,
Now memories, we hold so dear.

In this realm of dusk's soft light,
Hope finds shelter, pure delight.
Each step a whisper, calm and slow,
In the shade, our spirits grow.

Here, the past and present meet,
In this haven, wild and sweet.
Underneath these sacred trees,
We find solace in the breeze.

## Luminous Petals at Dusk's Door

In twilight's glow, the petals gleam,
Softly lit as if to dream.
Colors burst, a vibrant dance,
Nature's art, a sweet romance.

As day surrenders to the night,
These blossoms shimmer, pure delight.
Each moment holds a magic thread,
In the garden where we tread.

The fragrance drifts on evening air,
Entwining hearts, a gentle snare.
Luminous hues like stars unfold,
As dusk's embrace begins to hold.

A symphony of colors bright,
In silent whispers, pure and light.
Petals dance beneath the sky,
In this moment, time goes by.

As night descends, the blooms stay bold,
Their stories in the darkness told.
In every shade, a memory grows,
Luminous petals, night's sweet prose.

## Faerie Ferns and Moonbeam Dreams

In glades where faeries dance and twirl,
The ferns unfurl, a vibrant swirl.
Moonlight weaves through emerald fronds,
Creating magic in quiet ponds.

Whispers soft as shadows fall,
Ferns listen close, they hear it all.
Each night a story, wild and free,
In the realm of mystery.

Dreams take flight on velvet wings,
Chasing echoes of ancient things.
With every breeze, they swirl and sway,
In the starlight, they lightly play.

Faerie laughter sparkles bright,
In the hush of soft moonlight.
Ferns cast secrets in the dark,
Igniting every hidden spark.

As dawn encroaches on this dance,
Faerie ferns await their chance.
They weave a spell, serene and grand,
A world where dreams forever stand.

# Beneath the Canopy of Mist

Grey tendrils weave through trees,
Whispers dance on the breeze.
Shadows flicker, softly play,
Nature's secrets held at bay.

Footsteps hush on the ground,
Lost in silence, peace is found.
Glistening drops kiss the leaves,
A world stirs, as magic weaves.

Misty veils cloak the high,
Hidden paths beckon and sigh.
Guided by the heart's own light,
Into the dawn, out of night.

Ferns unfurl with mystic grace,
In their arms, a sacred space.
Eyes closed, hear the soft calls,
Of nature's language through the halls.

Beneath the boughs, dreams arise,
Cradled beneath the vast skies.
In the hush of morning's glow,
Life's sweet secrets start to flow.

## Enchanted Secrets of the Glade

Where sunlight dapples the earth,
Whispers tell of timeless birth.
In the glade, where shadows dart,
Echos linger, wild and smart.

Ancient trees with stories old,
Their gnarled barks, a tale untold.
Mossy carpets, soft and deep,
Guard the slumber, hush the sleep.

Dappled dances in the air,
Fleeting visions, scents so rare.
Every breeze a gentle sigh,
Footfalls light as spirits fly.

Wildflowers bloom with vibrant hues,
Painting paths with morning dews.
Hidden nooks invite the brave,
Secrets wait for those who crave.

In the glade's embrace, one feels,
Nature's magic softly heals.
With each step, the heart can sing,
Ancient truths the woods shall bring.

# Revelations of the Sylph's Sanctuary


In a glimmering, secret space,
Sylphs gather, light in grace.
Softly they weave the air,
With laughter bright and sweet as prayer.

Sunbeams dance on gentle streams,
Awakening forgotten dreams.
Petals drop like whispered notes,
Carried where the soft wind floats.

Rippling waters, crystal clear,
Reflect the wonder drawing near.
In their depths, the sylphs converse,
Through the current, they disperse.

With each flutter of their wings,
The sanctuary of magic sings.
Winds of change sweep through their play,
Revelations lead the way.

Mounting currents hold their grace,
Timeless tales all interlace.
In this haven, spirits soar,
Unlocking mysteries evermore.

## The Secret Language of Celestial Flowers

Amidst the gardens unfurling wide,
Celestial blooms, the universe's pride.
Petals brush against the skies,
In silence, they share secret ties.

Twilight whispers in colors bold,
Stories of the stars unfold.
Each blossom, a verse divine,
Crafted in the grand design.

Heavenly scents stir the night,
Under the moon's soft silver light.
In each flower's quiet grace,
Lives a universe to embrace.

Hidden meanings in their hues,
A language known by those who choose.
With fingertips, explore the lore,
Of blooms that speak forevermore.

In this garden, hearts connect,
To cosmic truths we seek to reflect.
Celestial flowers teach us all,
To rise with grace, to heed the call.

## Beneath the Sorceress's Façade


In shadows deep, her secrets lie,
A whisper soft, a knowing sigh.
Her eyes like stars, a captivating dance,
Beneath the silk, a furtive glance.

With every spell, she weaves a tale,
Of love and loss upon the pale.
Her laughter rings like chimes in air,
Yet in her heart, a muted care.

Through moonlit paths, she roams the night,
A sorceress cloaked in silver light.
The world around her breathes in grace,
But shadows linger, hiding face.

In glistening mist, she finds her way,
Where dreams and echoes fondly play.
Each step a promise, a thread of fate,
Weaving destinies before it's late.

Yet, beneath this charming guise,
Lies a heart that seeks the skies.
For in her magic, she yearns to be,
More than a tale, more than a sea.

# A Reverie Among the Ferns

In emerald depths, the ferns unfold,
A tapestry of green and gold.
Where time stands still, the heart takes flight,
In whispered breezes, soft and light.

A dreamer's path, so winding and sweet,
With nature's pulse beneath our feet.
The sunlight dances through the leaves,
In this embrace, the spirit weaves.

Each rustling leaf tells tales of yore,
Of tranquil streams and ancient lore.
With every step, the world feels near,
In ferns and dreams, we lose our fear.

Amidst the fronds, a silence sings,
A harmony of hidden things.
The heart, a compass, finds its way,
In reveries where shadows play.

Together, lost, we breathe the air,
A bond with earth, an answer rare.
Among the ferns, forever we dwell,
In nature's arms, all is well.

# Hidden in the Misty Grove

Hidden deep where shadows blend,
The misty grove waits for a friend.
Soft whispers rise, a gentle call,
In every corner, magic sprawls.

The trees wear veils of silver lace,
Guardians of a secret place.
In twilight's grasp, the stillness breathes,
As life among the shadows weaves.

With every step, the world hides coy,
A secret song, a fleeting joy.
The lanterns glow with fireflies' flight,
Guiding hearts through the soft night.

Among the roots where dreams collide,
The ancient spirits softly bide.
In every creak and rustle found,
The whispers of the lost resound.

Through misty veils, we find our truth,
In every shadow, the pulse of youth.
Together wandering, hand in hand,
In this grove, we make our stand.

# Songs of the Woodland Spirits

In twilight's glow, the woodlands play,
A symphony at close of day.
The spirits rise with gentle grace,
In every note, a warm embrace.

With rustling leaves and bubbling streams,
They weave the fabric of our dreams.
The softest sighs and laughter blend,
Echoing whispers that never end.

A dance unfolds where shadows glide,
In twilight's arms, they turn and hide.
From roots to boughs, their voices sing,
Of ancient tales and life in spring.

In every breeze, a magic swirls,
The hidden worlds and secret pearls.
Their songs invite both young and old,
To listen close, their stories told.

Through starlit nights, we find the way,
With woodland spirits, we shall stay.
Together bound in nature's song,
In harmony, where we belong.

# Petals Eloquent with Night's Embrace

In moonlit gardens, shadows play,
Soft whispers linger, drifting away.
Petals unfold, in silken grace,
Caressed by night, in a tender embrace.

Stars weave dreams in the velvet sky,
Each fragrant bloom, a soft sigh.
Dewdrops kiss the slumbering earth,
In their stillness, there's secret worth.

Time dances slow on this tranquil scene,
Where fragrance mingles, and hearts glean.
Owls serenade with a gentle hoot,
As night wraps the world in a dark blue suit.

Whispers of secrets in the cool breeze,
Nature's symphony brings heart's ease.
Petals fall like whispers of lore,
In the night, they promise to restore.

As dawn approaches, the hues ignite,
Petals close softly, losing their fight.
Yet in each fold lies a memory bright,
Eloquent petals, bathed in night's light.

## Delicate Whispers of the Eldergrove

Amidst the trees, where shadows dwell,
Whispers of wisdom begin to swell.
Leaves rustle softly in sacred dance,
Time holds its breath in a timeless trance.

Sunbeams filter through an emerald screen,
Nature's heart glows, vibrant and keen.
Mossy floors tell tales of the past,
Each gentle echo, a spell cast.

Ferns unfurl in the cool morning air,
Breezes carry secrets, gentle and rare.
In the stillness, the world finds peace,
Delicate whispers that never cease.

Beneath the boughs, life finds a way,
A vibrant tapestry where shadows play.
Old roots intertwine, stories implore,
Nature's canvas, forever to explore.

As twilight beckons, the grove sighs low,
A lullaby sung, in soft undertow.
Delicate whispers wrap around the night,
In the Eldergrove, all souls take flight.

## Faery Dances in the Fading Light

In the meadow where wildflowers bloom,
Faeries gather, casting off gloom.
Glimmers of laughter fill the air,
With wings of gossamer, light as a prayer.

Twilight descends with a magical flair,
Each faery twirls without a care.
Moonbeams sparkle on soft, silken grass,
As shadows mingle and moments pass.

Crickets serenade the dance of the night,
Flickering lanterns bring warmth and light.
The forest sighs under night's cool breath,
As faery songs defy the bounds of death.

In whispers exchanged, ancient tales reign,
Of love and longing, of loss and gain.
They beckon the stars to join their flight,
As dreams awaken in the softest light.

When dawn breaks softly, with hues aglow,
The faeries scatter, like dew, they flow.
Yet in the heart, their dance remains bright,
In memories held in the fading light.

## Twilight Blooms and Enchanted Veils

In twilight's grasp, the world holds breath,
Brushed by shadows, a dance with death.
Blooms unfurl beneath the waning sun,
Each petal whispers, a tale just begun.

Enchanted veils drift on the breeze,
Carrying secrets among the trees.
Soft colors blend, a painter's delight,
As day dreams linger into the night.

Mirrored in ponds, the sky begins to blush,
Night creaks softly, time feels the hush.
Mischief and magic in every glance,
Inviting all to join the dance.

Ancient spirits in the twilight sway,
Guiding the stars to light the way.
In whispered tales, hearts intertwine,
Among the blooming, the sacred divine.

As the last light fades, a promise made,
In twilight blooms, love won't ever fade.
Through enchanted veils, in dreams we'll roam,
Twilit whispers, they lead us home.

# Glimmers of Light in Verdant Havens

In the woodland whispers, light beams,
Dancing through leaves, like forgotten dreams.
Birds sing sweet melodies, soft and bright,
Painting the air with glimmers of light.

Moss carpets the ground, lush and deep,
Secrets of nature in silence we keep.
Sunlit pathways weave tales anew,
Guiding our hearts where the wildflowers grew.

Butterflies flutter on soft summer's breath,
A symphony played, life conquers death.
In the shade of the trees, shadows delight,
Embracing the warmth, we bask in the light.

Each step through the glen, where magic is found,
Echoes of laughter, a gentle sound.
Nature's embrace, a soothing retreat,
Glimmers of light beneath our feet.

Here in this haven, our spirits take flight,
Wrapped in the arms of the coming night.
With each fading sun, a promise we write,
In glimmers of love, our hearts shine bright.

## The Faerie's Veil of Fragile Dreams

In the moonlit glow, whispers take flight,
The faerie's veil shimmers soft and light.
Dew-kissed petals, a delicate scheme,
Woven with threads of a fragile dream.

Glistening laughter rings through the night,
In hidden glades, where shadows invite.
Secrets of time twirl in the air,
Stories of love, whispered with care.

Beneath ancient oaks, where wishes reside,
The fae gather close, their arms open wide.
In this realm where the restless hearts yearn,
Fragile dreams dance, and the world takes a turn.

Moonbeams cascade on the soft forest floor,
Each step draws us closer to magic's core.
In the stillness, our souls intertwine,
Chasing the remnants of dreams so divine.

As dawn's first light breaks the faerie's delight,
With whispers and giggles, they vanish from sight.
Yet in gentle sighs, the memories gleam,
The echoes remain of our fragile dream.

## Petals Falling like Stardust

In gardens where colors blend and play,
Petals fall lightly, drift away.
Each soft whisper carries a sigh,
Like stardust twinkling in the night sky.

Creating a canvas, vivid and bright,
Nature's artwork, a visual delight.
With every breeze, new stories unfold,
Secrets of petals in hues bold.

Time holds its breath as blossoms sway,
In the dance of the leaves, night turns to day.
Softly they scatter, a burst of grace,
Painting the earth with a gentle embrace.

Among the blooms, our dreams take flight,
Fleeting moments transformed by light.
In this magical realm where we trust,
We gather the petals, a treasure, a must.

As stardust dreams weave through the air,
With memories captured, we linger and stare.
Each petal that falls holds a promise concealed,
In nature's embrace, our hearts are healed.

# The Enchantment of Wild Blooms

In fields where wild blooms sway in the breeze,
The fragrance of freedom whispers through trees.
Colors collide in a vibrant display,
Nature's own canvas, an ongoing ballet.

Golden sunflowers reach for the sky,
With daisies dancing, they weave and they fly.
Each blossom a story, fragrant and bold,
Echoes of sunlight, in whispers retold.

Crickets provide a symphonic tune,
As twilight embraces the rising moon.
Underneath stars, wild dreams take their stand,
Elixirs of love in this wondrous land.

The enchantment of blooms, a spell we embrace,
Swaying together in nature's warm grace.
With laughter and joy, we tread on this path,
Awake to the magic, we embrace the aftermath.

As petals unfurl, letting go of their plight,
In the heart of the wild, everything feels right.
In the dance of the blooms, we find our own song,
The enchantment of life where we all belong.

## Whispers of Magical Petals

In twilight's soft embrace, flowers sigh,
Petals dance on whispers, dreams float high.
Colors blend like secrets, bold yet shy,
Nature's silent stories, under the sky.

Starlight bathes the garden in a glow,
In each bloom, the magic starts to flow.
Gentle breezes carry tales we know,
Through the night, the flowers put on a show.

A fragrant melody, sweet and rare,
Dewdrops glisten, sparkling everywhere.
In this realm of petals, none compare,
Hearts take flight, freed from all despair.

Each blossom holds a wish, a secret told,
In their quiet whispers, mysteries unfold.
A touch of wonder, a moment bold,
Wrapped in beauty, eternal and gold.

As dawn approaches, the magic fades,
Yet the memories linger in sunlit glades.
Whispers of petals, the heart invades,
In dreams, the enchantment never degrades.

## Enchanted Flora in Twilight Glades

In twilight glades, where shadows play,
Flora whispers secrets, night turns to day.
Colors shimmer softly, fading away,
In visions of magic, dreams softly sway.

Moonlit petals shimmer, gleam like stars,
Restless whispers carried on the breeze.
Nature's own symphony, free from bars,
In the heart of the night, the spirit frees.

Mystical fragrances float in the air,
Each bloom a story, a tale to share.
Magic entwined with the evening fair,
In the soft, sweet scents, we breathe the rare.

Dancing shadows, enchanting delight,
Each flicker brings forth a new aura bright.
In the quiet glades, we take flight,
Lost in the dreams of the silken night.

Awakening nature as dawn's light draws near,
Ethereal echoes dissolve with cheer.
The enchanted flora forever dear,
In memories captured, crystal clear.

# Beneath the Sylvan Canopy

Beneath the canopy, green and alive,
Whispers of nature in harmony thrive.
Branches weave together, a sheltering hive,
In this sacred space, dreams are contrived.

Sunbeams peek through, casting golden rays,
Caressing the ground in a soft, warm haze.
Leaves rustle gently, as if to praise,
The beauty of life in the forest's maze.

Moss carpets the earth, a plush, green bed,
Nature's embrace, where worries are shed.
In the woodland's heart, every path is led,
To secrets untold, where the curious tread.

Birdsong rings sweetly, a melodious chime,
Encouraging spirits to dance through time.
Underneath high boughs, life feels sublime,
Lost in the rhythm, a magical rhyme.

As twilight descends and shadows grow long,
The forest awakens with a haunting song.
In the sylvan haven, where we belong,
Beneath the canopy, the heart beats strong.

## Dreams Danced in Garden Shadows

In the garden's embrace, shadows entwine,
Dreams pirouette softly, sweet and divine.
Petals drip with twilight, colors combine,
In the hush of the night, magic's design.

Fleeting glimpses of fairies, mischief in air,
Whispers of laughter, they dance without care.
Moonlit reflections, a sight rare and fair,
In each crafted moment, beauty's laid bare.

The scent of the jasmine lingers so sweet,
As dreams take their flight on soft, padded feet.
In the quiet chaos, heartstrings entreat,
Embracing the night where enchantments meet.

The stars gaze down, a sparkling array,
As shadows weave stories in their ballet.
Dreams lost within petals, a soft sway,
Under the sky's watch, they gently play.

With dawn's approach, dreams begin to dissolve,
Yet memories linger, as hearts evolve.
In the garden's shadows, true magic resolves,
In the dance of the night, life's wonders revolve.

# Among the Winking Wildflowers

In fields where daisies dance with glee,
Beneath the sky, so wild and free.
They nod and sway in whispered cheer,
As butterflies flit ever near.

The sun dips low, a golden blaze,
Painting the world in vibrant hues.
A gentle breeze begins to play,
Carrying scents of morning dew.

Among these blooms, my heart takes flight,
Each petal shines, a jeweled sight.
In nature's choir, the silence sings,
A blissful balm that beauty brings.

Those wildflowers wink, secrets told,
In shades of pinks and yellows bold.
Each moment's grace, a fleeting spark,
Illuminating life from dark.

So let me roam through this sweet glade,
With wildflowers in playful parade.
Their laughter lingers, soft and bright,
Reminding me of pure delight.

# A Tapestry of Twilight Buds

As day transcends to starry night,
The twilight weaves a soft respite.
In gardens deep, the colors bloom,
A tapestry dispels all gloom.

The lavender sways in graceful rows,
While sleepy petals snuggle close.
The hush of dusk brings gentle peace,
Each bud a whisper, sweet release.

In twilight's hand, the echoes play,
Enchanting hearts in soft decay.
Each shadow holds a secret dream,
A world transformed, it all may seem.

Beneath the sky's deep indigo,
The stars arrive, they twinkle low.
Each tiny spark, a wish unspun,
A night of promise just begun.

So linger here, where silence breathes,
Amidst the twilight's gentle leaves.
In every bud, a dream is spun,
A tapestry when day is done.

## Gossamer Hues of Dusk


Through evening's veil, the colors rise,
In gossamer hues, the daylight sighs.
A brush of pink, a splash of gold,
As dusk unfolds, a sight so bold.

The horizon bleeds with twilight's grace,
Each stroke a story time will trace.
The clouds embrace the fading light,
Giving way to the approaching night.

With every shade, a memory gleams,
In quiet moments, lost in dreams.
The world wears a soft, tranquil guise,
While stars awaken in the skies.

As fireflies dance in gentle sway,
Marking the end of another day.
Their flickers weave a fleeting tale,
In dusk's embrace, we softly sail.

So pause and breathe this stunning view,
In gossamer hues, life feels anew.
With every sunset, there's hope unfurled,
A promise kept, our wondrous world.

# Echoes of the Sylvan Grove

In sylvan groves where shadows play,
The echoes of the day drift away.
Beneath the boughs, the whispers breathe,
Secrets wrapped in nature's weave.

A winding path through emerald trees,
Guided by the hum of busy bees.
Amongst the ferns, old tales reside,
In every rustle, life's soft tide.

The canopy holds a twilight dance,
As moonbeams slip through, a fleeting glance.
Each sound a story, each leaf a song,
In this rich realm, we all belong.

With every step, the heart aligns,
To rhythms sung by ancient pines.
The echoes linger, soft and low,
In sylvan nooks where spirits flow.

So wander deep in nature's care,
Feel every pulse, the tranquil air.
In echoes found, the soul may rove,
Forever held by the sylvan grove.

# Whispers of Enchanted Petals

In the hush of twilight's grace,
Petals dance with soft embrace.
Breath of roses, sweet and light,
Whispers twirl as day turns night.

Frogs croon near the water's edge,
Secrets shared without a pledge.
Moths flutter in silken attire,
Wings reflecting dreams on fire.

Stars peek through the leafy boughs,
Nature lanes make solemn vows.
Mirrored moon in stillness glows,
Whispers deep where magic flows.

Nightingale sings serenely sweet,
Harmonies in soft repeat.
In the garden, hearts entwine,
Touched by love, a kiss divine.

So, breathe in the fragrant air,
Find the magic resting there.
In whispers soft, let spirits soar,
Enchanted petals, forevermore.

# Secrets in the Garden's Glade

Hidden paths through gentle leaves,
Where time stops and nature weaves.
Sunlight dapples soft and rare,
Secrets whispered on the air.

Shadows dance with playful grace,
In this quiet, sacred place.
Each flower holds a tale untold,
In their colors, stories unfold.

Breezes sigh, a lover's call,
Nature's chorus echoes all.
Hidden laughter, echo sounds,
Joy resides in soft surrounds.

The brook babbles a tune of peace,
A moment's bliss that will not cease.
Butterflies, in bright display,
Guide the heart to find its way.

As shadows blend with fading light,
Secrets linger in the night.
In the glade, all fears subside,
Together in nature, we confide.

# Moonlit Blooms and Dreamer's Threads

Underneath the silver moon,
Flowers glow, a soft monsoon.
Dreams are woven in their light,
Filling hearts with pure delight.

Petals stretch like arms in prayer,
Crafting wishes on the air.
Whispers weave through night's embrace,
Moonlit blooms, a timeless grace.

Stars twinkle in velvet skies,
Casting dreams where hope resides.
Threads of silver, soft and bright,
Spin the stories through the night.

Time unfurls, a gentle thread,
In the garden, dreams are fed.
With each bloom, a promise made,
In moonlight, fears will soon fade.

As the dawn begins to break,
Awakened dreams, no more fake.
Moonlit blooms in morning's glow,
Carry whispers, seeds we sow.

# The Faery's Hidden Orchard

In a glade where shadows play,
Faeries dance in bright array.
Fruit hangs low, a tempting sight,
Glinted leaves in soft moonlight.

Nectar sweet, the honeyed air,
Whispers carried everywhere.
Magic drips from dew-kissed boughs,
Secrets sewn in quiet vows.

Petals gather 'round the tree,
In colorful fraternity.
Each blossom holds a tale alive,
Cradled here, they dance and thrive.

Gentle breeze, the faery's sigh,
Tales of heart and wild sky.
In this orchard, dreams collide,
With laughter echoing inside.

Time stands still beneath the stars,
Where the earth and magic are.
In hidden realms, our spirits roam,
In faery's love, we find our home.

# Tales of the Moonlit Flora

Under the silver gleam of night,
Whispers dance among the trees.
Petals glisten, soft and bright,
Nature's breath, a gentle breeze.

Crickets sing their midnight song,
As shadows softly stretch and sway.
In this realm, where dreams belong,
The world transforms, then slips away.

Glowworms light the winding paths,
Leading to secrets yet untold.
Each step unfolds the hidden laughs,
Of blossoms kissed by moonlight's gold.

Among the ferns, a tale unfolds,
Of heroes made of leaf and dust.
Their stories, timeless, brave, and bold,
In moonlit hours, they weave their trust.

So linger long beneath the sky,
And let the magic softly weave.
In the heart of night, reply:
The moonlit flora shall believe.

## Wandering Thoughts in Floral Breezes

In gardens where the wild winds play,
Thoughts drift along on petals' flight.
With each turn, a bright array,
Colors burst in joyous light.

Daisies nod with gentle grace,
Whispers of the day gone by.
Bees hum soft in this vast space,
Carrying dreams as they fly.

Butterflies on silken wings,
Dance through blooms of bright estate.
Each moment, new joy brings,
As nature weaves its gentle fate.

Lavender scents fill the air,
Soothing hearts with every breeze.
Lost in thoughts, without a care,
Time drifts as I roam with ease.

The sun dips low, a golden hue,
Casting shadows where I land.
In floral winds, my spirit flew,
Wandering thoughts, by nature planned.

### The Magic of the Hidden Flowerbed

In corners where the sunlight fades,
Lurks a secret, soft and rare.
With tangled roots and cool, dark shades,
A hidden flowerbed lies there.

Violets peek through blades of grass,
Glistening with the morning dew.
Nature's wonders as they amass,
Each bloom whispers a tale anew.

Soft petals cradle dreams in flight,
Every hue a promise made.
Hidden treasures bathed in light,
In this quiet, vibrant glade.

A soft breeze stirs the fragrant air,
As if to beckon hearts to see.
Magic thrives, with tender care,
In the flowerbed, wild and free.

So seek the whispers, find your bliss,
In corners where the shadows blend.
For in each bloom, a wondrous kiss,
The magic of life, without end.

# Hues of Light in the Blooming Tangle

In tangled lanes where blossoms twine,
Hues of light bend and unfold.
Amid the vines, sweet scents align,
A story of life, silently told.

Petals twirl in the soft wind's hand,
Every shade a note of song.
Glimmers dance on the vibrant land,
As daylight shifts and drifts along.

Dappled sunlight, a painter's touch,
Brushes blossoms, bold and bright.
Each hue speaks, it means so much,
In the blooming tangle of light.

Among the leaves, a secret lies,
A world unbounded, yet confined.
In petals' depths, where beauty sighs,
The heart finds solace intertwined.

So walk with wonder through this maze,
Let colors guide your path ahead.
In every turn, a moment stays,
In hues of light, where dreams are fed.

# The Glow of Hidden Flora

In twilight's hush, the flowers bloom,
Their secrets weave, dispelling gloom.
With petals bright, they softly sigh,
In whispered tones, they dance and lie.

Beneath the leaves, a shimmer grows,
A hidden world where magic flows.
In every shade, a story's told,
Of life and dreams, both brave and bold.

The dewdrops glisten, soft and clear,
They hold the wishes, hopes, and tears.
Each fragile stem, a tale to share,
Of love and loss, of joy laid bare.

As night descends, the stars appear,
They kiss the blooms with gentle cheer.
In silent vows, the life persists,
A symphony of nature's bliss.

So wander deep in nature's heart,
Where glow of flora plays its part.
With every step, discover more,
The magic held on hidden shore.

## Secrets of the Petal-Priestess

In twilight's grace, she walks alone,
A petal-priestess, by roots she's grown.
With every step, the blossoms wake,
Their vibrant hues, a path they make.

Amidst the ferns, she starts to chant,
To wild and free, the spirits grant.
In fragrant tones, her voice will rise,
Awakening dreams beneath the skies.

With sacred oils, she wields her art,
To heal the wounds, to mend the heart.
Each fragrant blend, a story spun,
Of ancient rites, of moon and sun.

Beneath her touch, the blooms will sway,
Their colors brightening the day.
In whispered prayers, they intertwine,
With secrets sung in every line.

The petal-priestess knows them well,
The hidden paths where shadows dwell.
In sacred woods, she finds her peace,
The dance of life, that will not cease.

## The Enchanted Garden's Embrace

In gardens graced by nature's hand,
A world unfolds, both bright and grand.
Where every flower sways with ease,
And whispers dance upon the breeze.

The colors burst, like laughter's song,
In harmony where hearts belong.
Each petal soft, a tender glow,
In twilight hours, the magic flows.

A hidden path where dreams convene,
Through verdant leaves, a sacred scene.
With every step, enchantment grows,
In every scent, the spirit knows.

The butterflies, like jewels in flight,
Weave through the blooms, a joyous sight.
In every corner, life pours forth,
The garden's heart, a source of worth.

Embraced by nature, souls explore,
The wonder found forevermore.
In this enchanted, sacred space,
We find our joy, our love's embrace.

# Whispers of the Lavender Vale

In lavender fields, the breezes flow,
With whispers soft, they breathe and glow.
The lavender blooms, like gentle sighs,
Awakening dreams beneath the skies.

The sun dips low, a golden hue,
As twilight wraps the vale anew.
In fragrant air, the magic spreads,
A tapestry where hope is fed.

Among the stems, the secrets lie,
In every color, a lullaby.
A soothing balm for weary hearts,
In every spray, a love imparts.

With every step, the spirits call,
In lavender's embrace, we find it all.
The moments linger, sweet and rare,
In whispers shared, a gentle prayer.

As night descends, the stars ignite,
In lavender vale, a world of light.
In dreams we wander, hand in hand,
In fragrant bliss, we make our stand.

## Curious Shadows on Petal Paths

Softly they dance in twilight glow,
Whispers of secrets among the flow.
Petals beneath, a canvas so bright,
Curious shadows play in the night.

Guided by beams of the silent moon,
Where flowers sway and nightbirds croon.
Each step reveals a hidden grace,
Mysteries whisper in this sacred space.

Through fragrant lanes, where dreams take flight,
Nature breathes life, casting pure delight.
In the hush of dusk, enchantments spill,
Shadows of wonder on every hill.

With each soft rustle, the night implores,
Embrace the beauty that nature stores.
Curious hearts follow the trail,
Chasing the remnants of a gentle gale.

Under starlit skies, together we'll roam,
In curious shadows, we'll find our home.
Paths painted bright by a floral art,
In this realm of wonder, we'll never part.

## The Blooming Heart of Fantasy

In gardens where wild dreams unfold,
Petals whisper tales of old.
Colors dance in a flawless blend,
The heart of fantasy begins to send.

Bees hum softly, weaving through,
Finding magic in every hue.
Butterflies wear crowns of light,
In this blooming heart, pure delight.

Morning dew on leaves does gleam,
A world awakened from a dream.
Each flower sings in gentle tone,
In their chorus, we're never alone.

With every breath, the spirit spark,
Guiding our souls through paths so stark.
In the blooming heart, love's gentle play,
Igniting fantasies day by day.

Join hands with breezes, let visions soar,
In this garden, forever explore.
Where fantasy flourishes, we'll always be,
Bound by the blooms of our reverie.

## A Tapestry of Floral Secrets

In the weave of petals, stories lie,
Colors entwined, reaching for the sky.
Each bloom a thread in nature's loom,
Binding whispers amidst the gloom.

Secrets held in fragrant blooms,
Shimmers of sunlight in shaded rooms.
A tapestry woven with care and grace,
Every stitch tells of time and place.

Roses blush with tales of love,
Daisies wink like stars above.
Tulips sway to the breezy dance,
Inviting us into a blissful trance.

To wander through this floral thread,
Is to discover the life we've led.
A sanctuary where souls connect,
Embracing each petal, we reflect.

So twist and turn through this floral maze,
In the tapestry bright, we'll forever gaze.
Every secret shared through bloom and sigh,
In nature's embrace, we learn to fly.

# Celestial Whispers in Verdant Halls

In the depths of greens where starlight gleams,
Celestial whispers weave through dreams.
Leaves lift high, cradling the air,
In verdant halls, magic is rare.

Moonlit paths of silver glow,
Guide our hearts where soft winds blow.
Every shadow holds a story told,
In whispers warming, never cold.

Branches sway with a gentle grace,
Inviting the stars to join the space.
Echoes of night dance through the trees,
Joining the symphony of midnight breeze.

Through this paradise, wander free,
In verdant halls, we'll always be.
Celestial secrets, softly shared,
In nature's embrace, we're forever paired.

So linger here beneath the light,
In the arms of darkness, find pure delight.
With every breath, let wonder sing,
In the verdant halls, our hearts take wing.